The Top 20 Public Companies in the Mobile Wallet Industry

By David W. Schropfer

Searching finance

Published under licence June 2014 by Searching Finance Ltd.

ISBN: 978-1-907720-73-4:

About the author

David W. Schropfer is an international business leader with two decades of management experience ranging from telecommunications to payment systems. Mr. Schropfer is the CEO of Anchor ID, Inc, and was previously a Partner with the internationally recognized consulting firm, The Luciano Group, where he led its Mobile Payment and Mobile Commerce practice. Earlier in his career, he was Senior Vice President with IDT Telecom, and a Business Development Officer for Capital One. He has served on the Board of Directors for multiple companies, and is a frequent speaker at industry conferences and trade shows. After graduating Boston College, David earned an Executive MBA from the University of Miami.

About Searching Finance

Searching Finance Ltd is a dynamic new voice in knowledge provision for the financial services and related professional sectors. Our mission is to provide expert, highly relevant and actionable information and analysis. For more information, please visit www.searchingfinance.com

Table of contents

Table of figures

Abstract

Abstract: Investing in mobile commerce is difficult because no pure-play companies have made it to the public market...yet. This world is changing everyday. What remains are other public companies that have been investing in businesses, and business divisions, that are focused on mobile commerce or mobile payments. Read this white paper to better understand which public companies are focused on this new sector, and how to avoid chasing the wrong opportunity in this rapidly changing environment.

Executive Summary

"The mobile commerce industry is primed for explosion around the world."

Pundits have been saying this for years.

Between 2015 and 2016, the era of mobile commerce will arrive. ANd it will be particularly disruptive, which will create potentially attractive opportunities, and crippling risk. Picking the winners and losers in any period of economic disruption is difficult. Monetizing the winners and losers can be even more difficult. Although there are many publicly traded companies that are already participating in mobile commerce, the winners are hard to find among the large and obvious failures.

Whether you believe mobile commerce will be a success, or failure, turning those convictions into a wise investment choices is difficult because most publicly traded companies do not exist completely within the mobile commerce space, which means you need to gauge the subset of a given public company's business model that can or will be affected by the mobile commerce industry.

The Worldwide Top 20

Hundreds of companies qualify as participants in the emerging 'mobile commerce' or 'mobile payments' industries. Many are worth watching for modest investment opportunity. However, only twenty are likely to translate into real investor value based on their mobile strategies.

Being on this list is not necessarily a good thing. In several cases, the liability of mobile commerce creates a significant problem to the future revenue of the organization. As indicated, some of these public companies stand to gain, and others stand to lose.

Best case and worst-case scenarios will only affect the subset of these public companies that are exposed to the mobile commerce industry.
This report separates those public companies   with *high opportunity* from those companies with *high exposure*. Ands this exposure can be good, bad, or managed. High exposure does not mean a company is going to lose revenue; rather it is an expression of risk or increasing risk due to the market pressures of mobile commerce and its competitors. In the same vein, companies with high opportunity in this report are not guaranteed to realize these new revenue dollars. Substantial execution is still required to capture market share, consumers, retailers adoption, and ultimately the revenue dollars suggested in this report.

Note that the chart on the following page indicates the top 15 companies that have the most to gain from mobile commerce, and the top 5 companies that have the most risk exposure due to mobile commerce.

Upside							Research

#	Category	Company name	Market	Symbol	Revenue (Billions)	% of buisness effected by MC	Future Index (Revenue Dollars Effected, Billions)
1	Manufacturers	Apple	NASDAQ	APPL	174	40%	13.9
2	Technology	Amazon	NASDAQ	AMZN	74	30%	11.1
3	Technology	Google	NASDAQ	GOOG	60	30%	9.0
4	Manufacturers	Samsung	Korea	KSE	213	30%	6.4
5	MNO	Sprint	NYSE	S	35	20%	4.9
6	MNO	AT&T	NYSE	T	128	5%	4.5
7	MNO	Verizon	NYSE	VZ	120	5%	4.2
8	Retail	Starbucks	NASDAQ	SBUX	15	20%	3.0
9	Retail	WalMart	NYSE	WMT	476	2%	2.9
10	Manufacturers	Verifone	NYSE	PAY	1.7	75%	1.3
11	Manufacturers	Ingenico	Paris	ING.PA	1.3	75%	1.0
12	Card brands	Discover	NYSE	DFS	8	100%	0.8
13	Retail	Target	NYSE	TGT	72	2%	0.7
14	Technology	Facebook	NASDAQ	FB	8	20%	0.6
15	Technology	twitter	NYSE	TWTR	0.7	10%	0.0

Downside							

#	Category	Company name	Market	Symbol	Revenue (Billions)	% of buisness effected by MC	Future Index (Revenue Dollars Effected, Billions)
1	Card brands	Amex (Serve & Bluebird)	NYSE	AXP	28	75%	-18.9
2	Card brands	Visa	NYSE	V	12	90%	-10.8
3	Card brands	Mastercard	NYSE	MA	8	95%	-6.8
4	Payments Industry	FIS	NYSE	FIS	6	75%	-3.2
5	Payments Industry	Fiserv	NASDAQ	FISV	5	75%	-2.6

Figure 1: List of all top 20 companies effected by mobile commerce index

The Company with the Biggest Potential for New Revenue: Apple

Apple has the potential to earn up to $14 billion in new revenue per year based on the new mobile commerce industry before 2018.

This makes Apple far and away the company most likely to benefit based on this analysis. That is another way of saying that Apple has nothing to lose, and everything to gain from the emerging mobile commerce industry. A closer look at the business lines reveals why.

Apple is expert at creating major revenue streams based on wholly new lines of business. Currently, its iTunes radio and Apple TV are two products that are entirely new revenue lines on their income statement, completely invented by Apple. Other new business lines of note in the last 10 years include the iPhone, and iPad.

So what can Apple due to maximize the potential of this new $14 billion in revenue? It starts by not reinventing the wheel.

Currently, Apple has approximately 300,000,000 credit card and debit card numbers on file for all of its iTunes purchases worldwide. Payments made on these credit cards rely on the standard credit card industry systems that the world has been utilizing for the last half-century. Apple wants to make it easy for customers to pay with these credit cards both online, and in brick-and-mortar retail environments. And it has the tools to do that. The iPhone, like other smartphones that came to market later, is a device packed with sensors. In addition to a microphone, camera, and cellular transceiver, the iPhone also contains a variety of radios, such as Bluetooth, Wi-Fi – even Global Positioning Satellite (GPS) systems are a type of radio. The trick is to use these radios in a way that allow the mobile device to securely communicate in the "near field," meaning that if a iPhone user wishes to let its iPhone communicate with another nearby computer, such as a retail cash register or loyalty registration device, the iPhone needs to be able to use one of its radios to do that.

The problem with these radios is that they each create a "back door" into the iPhone which can be used in an attack by a malicious computer. In

Name:	Apple, Inc.
Company Rank:	1: Biggest Potential Winner
Potential New Revenue from Mobile Commerce:	$14B/Year
Ticker Symbol:	APPL
Public Market:	NASDAQ
Key to Success	Maintain lock-out of competitors like Isis and Google Wallet, Leverage Secure Enclave and Biometrics (Touch ID's Fingerprint data) for security.

Figure 2: Apple Profile

some cases, without the user's knowledge, Bluetooth or Wi-Fi – for example – could be used for unauthorized access into an iPhone. This is why both of those technologies require active participation by the user to join a specific network for these technologies to function properly. For example, Bluetooth requires a "pairing" process where the user intentionally selects another Bluetooth device with which to pair and connect.

There are two new technologies in the marketplace today, one called Near Field Communication (NFC), and the other called Bluetooth Low Energy (BLE). Both of these technologies allow for mobile devices to be turned on without the knowledge of the user. This, obviously, creates an extremely significant problem: how does Apple secure its iPhone against unauthorized access through one of these technologies.

The mobile phone industry has answered the question by using something called a Secure Element, or SE. The SE essentially functions exactly like a smart card, and can secure a technology like NFC or BLE against unauthorized access.

But there is a problem with the Secure Element that stands between Apple and its $14 billion in new revenue. The problem is that the mobile network operator that the iPhone uses to connect to a cellular network, is actually the entity that owns the part of the phone (called a SIM card) where the Secure Element functions.

Unfortunately, the mobile network operators that own the SIM card have not provided reasonable access to other companies that want to utilize the Secure Element. Why are the mobile network operators ignoring this new potential revenue stream? Because the companies that want to use the Secure Element, like Apple or Google Wallet, are all competitors with a mobile wallet called "Isis" which is a joint venture between Verizon wireless, AT&T, and T-Mobile.

Given this competitive barrier, Apple took a close look at the SIM card, and realized that it is just another computer. A SIM card has a power source, processing capability, memory storage, and the ability to connect through a permission-based systems to other computers and applications. Apple, correctly, identified these elements as within its competence to build. Despite the mobile network operators threatening not to carry an iPhone that had a Secure Element built outside of the SIM card, Apple did just that – creating effectively a small computer within the iPhone which functioned like a SIM card solely for the purpose of managing Secure Element functionality, and not to authenticate a mobile device on a cellular network (which is the core and original function of the SIM card).

In the iPhone 5S, released in late 2013, Apple included an embedded Secure Element which it has elusively named the "Secure Enclave." Apple has not yet opened the Secure Enclave to developers, although Apple is using the Secure Enclave to secure the data related to the fingerprint data of Touch ID.

Currently, Touch ID is the name for Apple's new fingerprint hardware readers. On the iPhone 5S, a user can unlock the phone using only her fingerprint. Fingerprints are a form of biometrics, and fingerprint is a particular biometric form factor that has drawn some skepticism because, as one critic put it, "the fingerprint is a credential that you leave everywhere when you touch anything, and it cannot be changed."

It was the part about the fingerprint being, of course, unchangeable that raised concerns with Apple and potentially Apple's customers. If the fingerprint data was stolen by a fraudster, that fraudster would theoretically always be able to gain access to anything the victim accesses using their fingerprint as identification. To offset this concern, Apple announced that the data related to a user's personal fingerprint would (A) be stored in a Secure Enclave within the iPhone which was inaccessible by any other app or code running in the host memory of the device, and (B) never be transmitted from the phone in any way or stored in the 'cloud.'

To date, the sole function of the Secure Enclave is the storage of a user's personal fingerprint data. Nothing else. Companies that develop apps for iPhone's are expecting to eventually have access to this Secure Enclave, if only to ask it a binary question, such as, "did the user present a known fingerprint? Yes or no?" Theoretically, if the Secure Enclave entered the program with a simple "yes" then the app could rely on that answer as a form factor of security, thereby improving the user experience. But, Apple likes keeping closed systems closed whenever possible, so there is no guarantee they will open Touch ID to other developers.

For the purpose of payments however, Apple has two extremely interesting things they can do with the Secure Enclave, beyond just holding the fingerprint data. First, the Secure Enclave could be used to ensure that an NFC or BLE connection to the mobile device is authorized, much in the way that Isis uses the Secure Elements on the SIM card to get the necessary permission to an NFC chip functioning in the phone.

This is a remarkable game changer. If Apple uses the Secure Enclave for this purpose, it can have sole control over the BLE or NFC hardware, whichever is choosen to be put into future versions of the mobile device.

There has been significant debate around the question of why Apple has not yet installed NFC into any iPhones. Here are five reasons why that might be true:

1. Leverage available products, and other people's money (OPM). The Apple wallet is going to be called "Passbook." It works without an NFC chip, relying instead on geolocation to determine if an iPhone user is in the proximity of a compatible terminal. Geolocation is clearly not a permanent solution because it includes obvious problems, such as: unwanted notifications (if you ever want to be notified that you can use your Starbucks card, for example, you'll be notified whenever you can possibly use your Starbucks card, whether you want to or not), and imperfect functionality indoors (when you are in a shopping mall, GPS

has a hard time figuring out exactly where you are). There are no iPhone apps in the Apple App Store that support NFC, which makes sense since there has never been an iPhone that supports NFC. By contrast, there are dozens of applications that support QR codes and bar codes. Any iPhone app that displays a QR code for the purpose of being scanned by a terminal is a candidate for Passbook. The beauty of this model is that some company other than Apple has already paid to develop the QR/bar code processing, paid for training employees, and paid for scanning equipment needed at the point-of-sale. With all of this third-party investment in place, a company that wants to put their ticket/coupon/card into Passbook simply needs to load their information into the Passbook template. From there, it can take advantage of the key Passbook feature: opening from a locked screen.

2. Locked–screen access. Passbook opens from a locked screen. No third-party app can do that. Because Apple writes Passbook, it is integrated with the OS, which allows the app to open directly from a locked iPhone screen, straight to the scan-able code, which is a considerable advantage because it saves the user 2 to 4 steps per transaction.

3. The hardware and the battery: We know NFC technology takes up physical space within the phone, and uses power from the battery. Judging by the previous two points in this article, Apple is choosing to take advantage of systems and technology that have already been deployed. By not including an NFC chip in the iPhone 5 or 5S, Apple has time to figure out if it really wants to include an NFC chip in the next version of the iPhone, or possibly the version after that. If they choose to include NFC in a future version, they will have time to figure out where to squeeze in the NFC chip within the very crowded chassis of the 18% thinner iPhone 5 or 5S. Also, Apple is serious about maintaining long battery life between recharges, so they will want to ensure that the NFC chip does not use too much power. For example, consider Apple's deployment of 4G technologies. 4G has been around for years now, but the iPhone 5 is the first iPhone to include 4G compatibility. Why? According to a recent press conference, Apple wanted to make sure they could maintain a long battery life because 4G uses more power than 3G. So, if Apple was willing to wait over 2 years to get the customer experience right with 4G, it makes sense that they would be willing to wait to get it right with NFC.

4. Big Data Has to Start Somewhere: So why didn't Apple simply wait for an iPhone with NFC before it deployed Passbook? Understanding customer behavior with the mobile wallet is important in calculating what each customer is ultimately worth over time. Apple will begin collecting whatever data it can with the sale of the first iPhone; Apple will eventually be able to draw conclusions based on this data.

5. Buying a new iPhone is good for Apple: Many thought Apple would include NFC hardware in the iPhone 5 or 5S to allow for the option of a Passbook upgrading to NFC without requiring the user to buy a new

iPhone. But, since the iPhone 5 or 5S does not include an NFC chip, the customer is out of luck if Passbook evolves to support NFC in the future. Apple is unlikely to support a third-party micro-ST solution or a SIM card solution to NFC because Apple likes to control all of the hardware that is directly involved with its OS. So, buying a new iPhone will be necessary to support NFC. And, that is good for Apple. According to Apple's 10–K report released in late October last year, iPhone sales accounted for 43% of revenue. So creating an incentive for customers to buy another phone is a good thing to Apple. Even if all of the iPhone 5 or 5S buyers need to upgrade their phones in 2 years to take advantage of NFC, that fits into the average time it takes for an American user to upgrade their phone–which is about 22 months. So an upgrade in 2 years is unlikely to raise too much customer ire.

Regardless of the radio technology, Apple has a remarkable upside available to it through the emerging mobile commerce industry.

The Top 4 Potential Companies for New Revenue: Amazon, Google and Samsung

Other than Apple; Amazon, Google, and Samsung rated highest on the mobile commerce opportunity scale. Each of these three companies earned a rating of roughly 30% in terms of the percentage of their existing business that could be positively affected by mobile commerce, but all three for very different reasons.

In the case of Amazon, their potential to increase sales through "show rooming" is highly significant. Show rooming is the practice of the consumer shopping for a particular products on the shelf of a bricks and mortar retail store, while using their mobile phone to research a lower price for the same item at another retailer. Due to its low cost of shelf space (all Amazon products are stored in a warehouse) Amazon is highly capable of competing on price. Add to this advantage the fact that Amazon is one of the largest payment mechanisms on the Internet, with tens of millions of credit card numbers on file, and Amazon can offer better price, instant selection, and seamless payment all through a mobile wallet app. This is a compelling prospect, and the reason I believe Amazon could realize up to $11.1 billion in new annual revenue to the mobile commerce industry over the next several years, as big-box retailers continue to battle this competitor.

Google Wallet is clearly capable of being a front runner, although there really are no front runners for the nascent industry of mobile wallets because adoption is presently so low. Google Wallet may or may not have the marketing messaging, product design, or commitment to convince tens of millions of users to adopt their mobile wallet product. That problem remains to be solved. The problem that seems to have been solved is that of addressable market. As of February 2014, the full Google Wallet product is only available in the United States on the Sprint mobile network (17% of the US mobile market) and on less than half of Sprint users that use an iPhone, which leaves a scant 7% of the US mobile market as Google Wallet's addressable market. When Google Wallet integrates Host Card Emulation, it could access more than 50% of the US Mobile market within the time it takes Android users to upgrade from their existing version of Android to Android 4.4 (KitKat).

The iPhone could be a problem for Google Wallet until Apple decides to include NFC in its phones. But the possibility exists that a combination of Bluetooth low energy (BLE) and Host Card Emulation could give Google Wallet a way to communicate from an iPhone app directly to a point-of-sale device.

Google Wallet, Isis, and other mobile wallets have a long way to go before they earn consumer trust and confidence. But the basis of their business model is sound because it adds convenience to the user experience. The technology is sound because it is based on smart cards, which have trillions of use-cases proving their efficacy. Host Card Emulation is young, and unproven in the mass-market at present. But, if it is proven to be better then any other form of encryption, which is possible, then it will quickly change the availability of these wallet products in the marketplace, and Google Wallet stands a fighting chance of gaining the market-dominating position it seeks.

Samsung has a very different model, and an interesting opportunity with a technology called Embedded Secure Elements. Almost all mobile wallets seek to have easy access to a radio for ingress and egress between a mobile device and point-of-sale system. These technologies include Near Field Communication (NFC), Bluetooth Low Energy (BLE) and Wi-Fi. In each of these cases, securing and protecting these radio transceivers with a secured encryption key is critical in preventing malicious attacks. So far, the only Secure Element available installed on mobile devices is in the SIM card, which is owned by the mobile network operators and not easily accessed at any price. Samsung, however, recently launched an experiment in Australia to see if it could effectively host the smart card hardware within the motherboard of one of its mobile devices. The experiment is functioning properly, but is already at a roadblock; the mobile network operators in the United States threatening to prohibit Samsung from selling this particular feature in the United States. This could take decades to play out through the FCC, the SEC, and the DOJ in the United States. In the meantime, the mobile carriers will enjoy an advantage.

Regardless, Samsung has the opportunity to provide a unique suite of security services to app developers and others around the world, creating a remarkable new category of income for Samsung which could reach into the billions within the next several years. Our estimate is that this figure will reach US$6.4 Billion in new revenue by 2018.

The Company with the Greatest Risk: AMEX

AMEX is at the bottom of our list. Let's be clear about what that means. Being on the bottom of our list means only that there is far more downside than upside in terms of revenue potential. Based on our analysis, there is very little that AMEX can do to create new lines of revenue. However, there is significant opportunity for AMEX to lose gross revenue dollars in its existing lines of business. In other words, mobile commerce is not going to help AMEX to grow; in fact AMEX have to work hard to maintain its existing level of revenue.

While AMEX is exposed to a significant loss in revenue, it does not mean that that will happen. In fact, AMEX is already making some excellent strategic moves to keep on the right track. For example: in 2013 AMEX announced that it would allow free cash reload reward of its stored value products at up to 70,000 retail point-of-sale locations in an effort to better serve the un-banked and under banked populations. Attempting to win new customers in the under banked and un-banked consumer segments is a smart way for AMEX to offset some of the risk that it is experiencing elsewhere in its business lines.

The biggest factor that contributed to AMEX's low rating in this analysis is that all of its business lines are exposed to new business lines which will be enabled by mobile commerce. Which means there's nowhere to hide. A central thesis of the emerging mobile commerce industry is that the ability for smart phone to connect to any other machines through the Internet, and the ability for a typical retail point-of-sale device to connect to any machine via the Internet, means that the large, expensive, legacy systems built during the course of the last 60 years may be eclipsed by newer, more agile, and less expensive platforms. Logically, the company running a less expensive platform will have a lower incremental cost of operations, and therefore a competitive advantage against legacy companies. We already see this happening with companies like PayPal enjoying extremely low

Name:	American Express Company
Company Rank:	1: Biggest Potential Loser
Existing Revenue	
Potential Revenue Loss from Mobile Commerce:	$19B/Year
Ticker Symbol:	AXP
Public Market:	NYSE
Key to Minimizing Loss	Focus on New lines of business like Serve/Bluebird. Partner aggressively with other mobile wallets. Lead in P2P market. Stick to existing Value Add – member benefits.

Figure 3: AMEX Profile

cost of sales and operational expenses related to how it moves some (but not all) of its funds between its members.

So what key strategic moves that AMEX can make to stave off disaster? Here are a few:

- Focus on new lines of business including Serve/Bluebird.
  These new products from American Express are a direct attack on traditional banks and credit unions. They replace the traditional checking account in a number of ways; including electronic bill payments, online access to statements and balances, free Direct Deposit from most paycheck and payroll companies, free AT withdrawals at over 23,000 ATM, subaccounts for children or other needs, and other items including no minimum balance. A user can even deposit a check into their Serve account using only the camera on their smartphone, a feature called 'remote check capture.' The fee for Serve is one dollar per month, which will be attractive to even low income households based on the services.

FREE Cash Reloads at the Register

At over 15,000 CVS/pharmacy® stores & participating 7-ELEVEN® locations

Add cash for FREE at over 15,000 CVS/pharmacy® and participating 7-ELEVEN® locations. Just give your cash and your American Express Serve® Card to the cashier and your money is immediately added to your Card.

Visit **serve.com/addcash** to find cash loading locations in your area.

serve®   Your Full Service Reloadable Prepaid Account

08-03659-010

Figure 4: Serve Flyer Sent to Customers in January, 2014

- Partner aggressively with other mobile wallets.
  Here, AMEX has done an excellent job. They not only have partnered with Isis, the joint venture between Verizon wireless, AT&T, and T-Mobile, but this Serve card is actually the stored value mechanism within Isis mobile wallet. Isis has a significant problem in that it can only directly support only three financial institutions, including American Express, Chase, and Wells Fargo. A credit card or debit card issued by any other financial institution cannot be loaded directly into the Isis Wallet. Instead, the holder of a credit or debit card from another financial institution must link it to the American Express Serve card as a source of funds. That means when the Isis user makes a purchase using the Serve card in the Isis mobile wallet, the funds will be pulled automatically from the user's credit or debit card. This is a complex, but

essential mechanism for Isis because, without it, the Isis mobile wallet would be closed to anyone that did not hold an account with American Express, Chase, or Wells Fargo. Capital One was a early supporter of the Isis wallet, but pulled out in September 2013.

■ Lead in P2P market.
The peer-to-peer product is not a revenue – generating product for AMEX or Serve. This is really a "me too" feature that allows AMEX server to be competitive with other products, such as Google Wallet. The cost to deliver this value approaches zero on an incremental basis, so it is really simply a value-added feature that allows Serve to be more competitive.

The good news for AMEX is that they appear to be doing all of these elements, and doing them well. There is no scenario where AMEX comes out ahead after the impact of mobile commerce has come and gone, based on this analysis, or at least it is extremely unlikely. However, the possibility exists that AMEX can maintain its current level of revenue for a long time to come.

The Rest of the Top 3 with Greatest Risk Exposure

Visa and Mastercard round out the top three most exposed companies due to Mobile Commerce. Absurd? Maybe not. Visa, MasterCard and AMEX and their peers are acknowledging a serious threat in the future: the Smartphone. All of these companies make their money by taking a very small percentage of every transaction that uses their services. But what if you could complete a transaction without their services? What if you could walk into any store, restaurant, doctor's office, or hot dog stand and buy something without using their services? What is the alternative, and who are the potential players that could make it happen?

Visa, MasterCard and American Express (a.k.a. AMEX) are the three dominant players in the payment system that enables you to use the credit cards and debit cards in your wallet today. The system is complex, but very mature: On one side, consumers want credit cards so they go to businesses called "issuers." An issuer is typically a bank, credit union, or other company like Capital One (before they started buying traditional banks). Of course, it costs money to issue your card and manage your account, and most of these institutions also like to make a profit (credit unions do not make a profit), so issuers charge you interest and fees to make money.

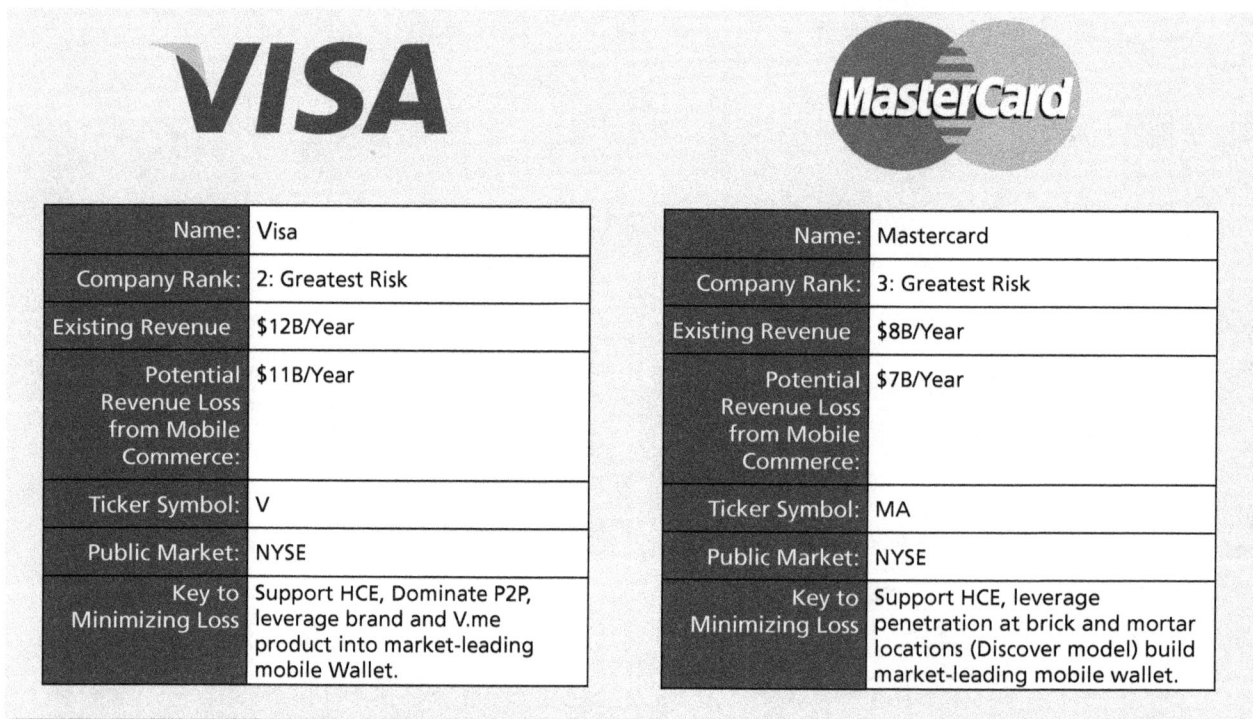

Name:	Visa		Name:	Mastercard
Company Rank:	2: Greatest Risk		Company Rank:	3: Greatest Risk
Existing Revenue	$12B/Year		Existing Revenue	$8B/Year
Potential Revenue Loss from Mobile Commerce:	$11B/Year		Potential Revenue Loss from Mobile Commerce:	$7B/Year
Ticker Symbol:	V		Ticker Symbol:	MA
Public Market:	NYSE		Public Market:	NYSE
Key to Minimizing Loss	Support HCE, Dominate P2P, leverage brand and V.me product into market-leading mobile Wallet.		Key to Minimizing Loss	Support HCE, leverage penetration at brick and mortar locations (Discover model) build market-leading mobile wallet.

Figure 5: Profiles of Visa and MasterCard

On the other side of the spectrum, restaurants, stores, and other merchants want to accept your credit card as a payment for their goods and services. To do that, they go to companies called "acquirers" which typically provide a device or software for merchants to accept your credit card as payment. As part of the acquirers service, they do some of the backend processing that delivers an approval code to the merchant at the time of purchase to ensure that your card is good and your bank will pay. But, all that costs money, so the Acquirer charges fees to the merchant. These fees include something called "interchange" fees, which means that a percentage of the transaction amount will be kept by the acquirer and not paid to the merchant, typically about 1.5% to 4%. Another type of fee is a transaction fee, which is typically a fixed amount of money that the merchant pays the issuer regardless of the amount of the transaction, usually between $.20 and $.50 and $.50 per transaction. In the middle of issuers and acquirers is the core of the payment system. These include Visas computers, MasterCard's computers, etc. since every acquirer does not want to have a direct relationship with every issuer, both camps use Visa, MasterCard, etc. as the intermediary.

The market pressure to lower the cost of this system is real. Most notably from PayPal and MCX (a joint venture between many of the major retailers in the US). MCX is building an alternate payment channel to MasterCard and Visa. The MCX product relies on the mobile device to generate a payment directly from the customers checking account to the checking account of the retailer. The money transfer will likely run over ACH rails, more commonly known as 'wire transfer' services. Even startups like Dwolla, which is an alternate payment method at a fraction of the cost of Visa and MasterCard, presents a model that is troubling to Visa and MasterCard and attractive to retailers.

But, Visa, MasterCard, and American Express have one thing that the startups don't have: almost 60 years of combating fraud. Collectively, these companies have pooled their knowledge of fraud techniques and come up with a standard known as PCI, or payment card industry, which outlines the specific audit required to ensure that retailers are in compliance with the rules and regulations designed to combat the real world fraud experience that these companies have learned over time.

Regardless, Visa and MasterCard will need to work hard to ensure long-term survival. Their legacy platform, and expensive processes will need to be streamlined in the future if they are to stem the threat of these newcomers. Visa and MasterCard's mobile leaders, Bill Gadja and James Anderson respectively, are well-tenured and experienced leaders who are making extraordinary efforts to lead their companies through the turbulence of the mobile payment industry birth.

Gadja was a former head of the GSM Association (GSMA), and was tapped to lead Visa's efforts because of his extraordinary connections within the mobile network operators around the world. And, Visa needs the carriers' cooperation because the carriers own the most secure part of the payment transaction on a mobile device; the SIM card. Unfortunately for Mr. Gadja, the mobile network operators have proven to be difficult to work with because they have invested in a competing wallet model with a company called Isis. Thankfully, a new technology was born recently that MasterCard and Visa have both chosen to support.

In February 2014, Visa and MasterCard declared their support for Host Card Emulation for payment processing. Host Card Emulation is an extremely young technology. It was invented in 2011 by the founders of SimplyTapp, Doug Yeager and Ted Fifelski in Austin, Texas. The first commercial release was only a year later on August 29, 2012. But the biggest endorsement came in November 2013 when Google released Host Card Emulation integrated with its new Android 4.4 operating system release called Kit Kat.

In short, Host Card Emulation may supply Visa and MasterCard with an alternative to working directly with the mobile network operators, opening the potential for these companies to have a remarkably competitive products, and again, mitigate the risk.

About the Rating System

This rating system contains three critical components: Existing Revenue; Percentage of business exposed to mobile commerce, and our proprietary calculation of the extent to which a particular company's business will be effected by mobile commerce (maximum of 1, and minimum of -1). These three figures are multiplied together to create an estimated opportunity or risk assessment measured in US dollars.

Summary and Conclusion

Measuring the winners and losers is a difficult proposition. Success and failure in the mobile commerce industry is going to depend on several unpredictable factors, such as the capabilities of the management team, the continuing commitment by the corporation, competitive steps and missteps, and plain dumb luck. I have not attempted to identify what products consumers will adopt and retailers will embrace; instead I have detailed risk where risk exists and opportunity where opportunity exists, and attempted to measure these in dollars.

www.ingramcontent.com/pod-product-compliance
Lightning Source LLC
Chambersburg PA
CBHW051235200326
41519CB00025B/7390